IMAGES
of America

AFRICAN-AMERICAN LIFE
IN
JACKSONVILLE

IMAGES
of America

AFRICAN-AMERICAN LIFE
IN
JACKSONVILLE

Herman "Skip" Mason, Jr.

ARCADIA

First published 1997
Copyright © Herman "Skip" Mason Jr., 1997

ISBN 0-7524-0883-6

Published by Arcadia Publishing,
an imprint of the Chalford Publishing Corporation,
One Washington Center, Dover, New Hampshire 03820.
Printed in Great Britain

Library of Congress Cataloging-in-Publication Data applied for

*I dedicate this book
to the memories of my deceased grandparents,
Henry and Lola Harris and James and Elizabeth Mason,
and my great grandmother Pearl West,
a phenomenal African-American woman
who owned property in Fernandino Beach, Florida, operated a "jook joint,"
and understood the importance of economic prosperity
long before it became fashionable for African-American women.*

Contents

Preface

African-American Life in Jacksonville is the most comprehensive pictorial history of Jacksonville's African-American population since 1926. It was then that Reverend Thomas H.B. Walker wrote *The Story of the Negro in Jacksonville: From Pioneer Days to the Present, a Negro Blue Book Publication.*

This new book of Jacksonville's African-American life and events between the late 1800s and the 1950s should enhance the information found in earlier publications and bridge the gap between the known and the unknown. This pictorial history should educate all segments of Jacksonville's population concerning the tremendous and outstanding contributions that the African-American population made during those decades. It should also dispel the myths and images of all or most of Jacksonville's African Americans as being shiftless, lazy, and crime prone. Instead, it should tell the story of industrious, productive, caring, law-abiding people who struggled to overcome oppression, disfranchisement, and poverty. Their progressiveness and success should be evident in the number and quality of their businesses, professions, and religious, educational, fraternal, civic, and social institutions and organizations which they developed.

The author and collector of images, Herman "Skip" Mason Jr., spent several years interviewing, researching, identifying, and processing hundreds of photographs for inclusion in this book. Many of the images were taken by Mr. E.L. Weems, considered to be Jacksonville's foremost African-American photographer from 1929 to the late 1970s. His camera caught events such as weddings, graduations, and social, civic, religious, and education events, as well as individual and family portraits. Mason coordinated photographs with historical facts into a tapestry of Jacksonville's rich African-American heritage. This work should be an invaluable source of reference for the present generations and also for future generations.

Camilla Perkins Thompson
Historian

Forward

Who among us would not want a pictorial history of the very community in which you were born, went to the first grade, and did at least some of the things your parents told you not to do? Wouldn't you love to have a second chance to see some of the news clippings that your folks didn't bother to save? Of course pictures have a way of reminding you—often by what is not portrayed—of what was wrong about your hometown, as well as what was so special about growing up there.

Thanks to this work by Skip Mason, all African Americans and I who knew Jacksonville between the 1920s and the 1950s now have splendid reminders of our part of town.

I delight in seeing this book's people and places that were so much a part of my early life. But there is so much for everyone in this pictorial history of my hometown—even if you never drank a big grape pop at Mr. Broadnax's filling station, strained to hear grown-ups gossip about what was said to have happened to Ashley Street, or felt a deep sense of pride every time you walked into the Afro-American Life Insurance Company. That is because Skip Mason has used the splendid photography of Ellie Weems to capture that which was specific about Jacksonville, Florida, but also what was universal in the experience of the Black folks in the Deep South during a period of intense segregation.

Here is a book that, far more vividly than a million words, points the way for us Black folks from Jacksonville. After all, you can't know where you're going if you don't know where you've been.

Johnnetta B. Cole

One

Familiar Streets

Ashley Street:
"It was Jacksonville's Answer to Harlem"
Frank Pearson
Feb. 1, 1991

Every major city has a street of prosperity, a street bustling with businesses, such as restaurants, barber and beauty shops, night clubs, and theaters. For blacks in Jacksonville, that street was Ashley Street. The Strand Theater (now demolished) offered vaudeville shows and movies during its run on Ashley for over fifty years. By 1915, there were five theaters: the Air Dome, Globe, Frolic, Strand, and later, the Roosevelt Theater, all located on Ashley Street.

The street was so popular that Paramount Recording Company artist Leola B. Wilson recorded a song titled "Ashley Street Blues" in 1926.

Ashley Street was known for its restaurants and cafes, including Hayes Luncheonette (above), at 634 Ashley Street, c. 1938, owned by Georgia Wilson and Gibbous Hayes, and Campbell Cafe (below), c. 1949, owned by Gussie Campbell. Both have since been demolished.

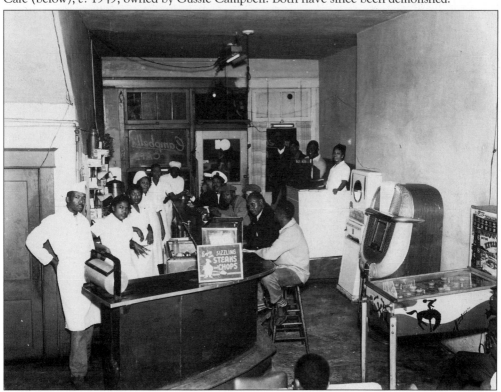

Eartha Mary Magdelene White recognized in her life the need to provide services for the homeless, indigent, orphans, and others who were in need. By 1908, she was operating out of a house on Eagle Street (now First Street). She founded the Clara White Mission in 1921 and named it for her mother, who died in the same year. The mission distributes food and clothing, provides shelter, and helps find employment.

In 1932, the Clara White Mission moved to 611–613 W. Ashley Street into this 1912 building owned by Frank Crowd. It had previously been the Globe Theater, a Mercantile Company, and a hotel. After a fire in 1944, the building was completely renovated for $65,000. H.J. Klothuo was the architect and O.P. Woodcock served as contractor. Afro-American Life Insurance Company provided a $33,000 mortgage for the project. The mission still remains at this location.

The Willie Smith Building on the corner of Ashley Street and Broad Street housed the Florida Cut Rate Pharmacy and the Hollywood Music Store. Though the businesses have closed, the building still remains.

A popular pastime was hanging out in the music department of the Hollywood Music Store, founded in 1924. The store, pictured here c. 1949, was owned and operated by Joe Higdon, a popular dance promoter who, along with Frank Usher, brought major entertainment acts to the city. Higdon, a native of Thomasville, is shown with employees of the store. He died in 1958, and his cousin, local musician Nathaniel Small, inherited the store.

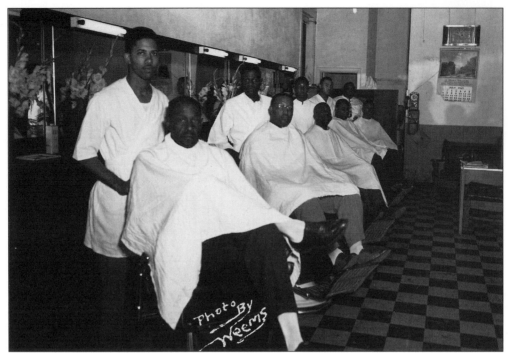

Barber and beauty shops were frequent in number near Ashley Street, including the Roosevelt Barber Shop, which opened in 1946 and is still in operation. The shop was located in the Clara White Mission Building. Pictured standing, from left to right, are: Ralph Tisdale, unidentified, unidentified, Cephus Thompson, and Nathaniel Roger (barber shop owner). Seated, from left to right, are Mr. Steve, Willie Smith, unidentified, Jerome Singleton, and unidentified, c. 1947.

Located in the 600 block of West Ashley between Broad and Jefferson Streets were the Hotel Eggmont; Brad's Cafe; the Artistic Barbershop; the popular Manuel's Tap Room, owned by Manuel "Chula Papa" Riveria; John Betsch Place; and Carl and Daisy Ford's Bubber's Coffee Shop. All have since been demolished.

The Florida Tattler, published by Porsher Taylor, was just one of many newspapers published in Black Jacksonville. Others were the *Florida Sentinel*, edited by Lemuel Butler in the 1920s and published by C. Blythe Andrews, and the *Jacksonville Progressive News*, published by Susie Brown. *The Jacksonville Journal* included a "Colored News Section" which was edited by Beulah McClellan until 1959, when it was moved to the *Florida Times Union*. Uriah Portee was the first black reporter for the paper. In 1951, Eric Simpson began publishing the *Florida Star*. The office burned to the ground in 1993, and after Simpson's death, his wife continued the operation.

A Prosperous & A Happy New Year

The Fla. Tattler - 2c

The Tattler is published weekly,and is selling for 2c per copy.

Vol. 1   JACKSONVILLE, FLA., SATURDAY, DEC. 29, 1934   No. 20

Firestone Employes Mob and Beat New Deal Cab Driver and Owner

Read Story On Page 4 and 5

The Late Bessie Coleman, Died In Service For The Cause.

Life of Bessie Coleman

COURTESY JOE JAMES, JR.

Bessie Coleman, born in 1896, in Atlanta, Texas: 12th child of 13 children.

During the World War, she became interested in Aviation — she worked laborously to save enough money to complete her course. She went to Europe to enter The ondrome school of Aviation, and finished in 1920.

She returned to America in 1921— went back to France to gain additional technique which carried her in to Germany, Belgium and many other Foreign Countries. She was Certified in Germany and France, which gave her an International Pilot's License.

She was the first of her race to become a Licensed Pilot She was the first American woman to receive a pilot's license from Germany.

She came to Florida in 1925, and made her headquarters in and around Orlando. She owned her plane, and while arranging for the May Day Celebration, under the auspices of the Jacksonville Negro Welfare League, she was killed at Paxon Field on Friday morning, April 30, 1926, with her Co-pilot. William D. Willis, also of Texas Bessie was 30 yrs. old at death Last Rites in Orlando, May 2, 1926. Interment in Chicago, Ill.

Julius Henderson (far left) was a longtime employee of the Strand Theater and also managed at one time the Club Tomoka. He is shown with with Mrs. Arnolta Williams, a resident of Jacksonville since 1918 and the social columnist for the *Jacksonville Telegraph* and a correspondent for *Jet Magazine*, the *Pittsburgh Courier*, and the *Chicago Defender* newspaper; and Arv K. Rothchild, owner of the Strand. Other National Theater employees not pictured are Eugene Watson and Richard McKissick of the Roosevelt Theater.

Before the construction of the Knights of Pythias Building, the fire of 1901 destroyed several large halls, including the Odd Fellows, Parkers Hall, the Good Templars, and the Masonic Building. It was rebuilt at 727 W. Ashley Street and included a hotel, boarding rooms, meeting rooms, and a string of storefront business, such as Dr. James P. Patterson's Drug Store, Sentinel Publishing, White Front Pool Parlor, and Peoples Dressmaking Shop. A dance hall was located on the third floor where major entertainers performed. The Daughters of Calanthe also met in the building. This structure was demolished in 1957. Plans to construct a hotel/apartment replacement were never realized.

Customers wait inside of the Eutopia Beauty Shop on W. Ashley Street. The shop was owned by Callie Johnson, *c.* 1942.

The Jenkins Radio Repair Shop, operated by Samuel Jenkins, was also located on W. Ashley Street, *c.* 1945. It was known as the "Voice of Ashley Street." When the shop closed, Manuel Rivera then opened and operated a confectionery store, now demolished.

Located on the corner of Jefferson Street and W. Ashley Street, the Finkelstein Building, which housed a number of businesses, still stands. From the turn of the century to the 1950s, this building was home to the popular Lenape Bar, which marked the era of swing music and the Jazz Age for blacks in Jacksonville. The building was constructed in 1895 by Sebastian Genovar as a grocery store and it later became a boarding house. Then, Cora Taylor bought the dilapidated boarding house and opened a nightclub and bordello called the Hotel de Dreme, which was located across the street from the Strand Theater. From the 1920s to 1940s, the building became a haven for musicians, like local musician Cootie Williams, who would go on to play for Duke Ellington's band. In 1931, the Wynn Hotel opened and entertainers such as Louis Armstrong resided there. During the 1940s, in front of the Lenape Bar, there were two metal horse-hitching rails known as the "rail of hope." Musicians and waiters often hung out there waiting for a job.

The Broadnax Service Station opened in 1922 and was located at 816 W. State Street, directly behind the Ritz Theater. It was owned and operated by J.A. Broadnax, a graduate of Howard University who acquired the business from his uncle in 1929. It was demolished in 1995.

Two

"Out East"
on Florida Avenue

Originally known as Oakland at the turn of the century, the area east of what was Florida Avenue to African Americans in that area is known as the Eastside. It was home to a thriving black middle class, including the family of architect R.L. Brown and the Hurstons, Blanch, John Hurston, and their daughter Zora Neale Hurston, who resided on Evergreen Avenue for a short period time. Other families included the Latsons, Ervins, Daniels, Browns, and Vaughts. Florida Avenue was renamed A. Phillip Randolph Boulevard. Schools in the area were the Franklin Street and Oakland Elementary Schools and the Matthew Gilbert School, which was built in 1926 and originally called the Old Maysville Road School.

One of Eastside businesses was the Florida Pharmacy at 1230–32 Florida Avenue. The store was owned by Willie J. Smith and opened in 1939; it also offered free delivery to customers, c. 1945.

Young men learned the skill and art of tailoring at Fred Richardson's Tailoring Shop located at the Eastside. Other specialty shops included Brooks Shoe Store, Oscar Mathis Shoe Store, Buster Ford's Restaurant, Anderson Cafe, Ann's Cafe, and the Pix Theater, c. 1946.

Mr. Benjamin Gamble owned and operated a grocery store on Florida Avenue.

This building housed the Peoples Burial Company and the Simmons Dry Cleaning Shop. It was located on 915 East Union Street.

The Foremost Dairy deliveryman made daily deliveries of fresh dairy products to his customers.

In 1924, Sophia Starks Nickerson founded the first licensed beauty culture school in the state of Florida. When the school was in its prime, it trained hundreds of women, who were required to have over a thousand hours of operating time.

Nickerson's was located at 1503 North Myrtle Drive.

James Mason, a native of Hazlehurst, Georgia, came to Jacksonville in the 1920s and found work as a boot black at the Hotel Burbridge Barbershop (above) on Forsyth and Clay Streets, where he worked for over thirty years. He and his family resided on W. Ashley Street.

In 1901, A.L. Lewis, along with Rev. J. Milton Waldron, Rev. E.J. Gregg, E.W. Latson, A.W. Price, James Franklin Valentine, and Dr. Arthur Walls Smith, met in Rev. Waldron's parsonage and organized what would become the Afro-American Life Insurance Company. Two years later, the Afro-American Pension Bureau was organized. The building was located

on the corner of East Union Street and Ocean Street. Presidents of Afro-American were: Rev. E.J. Gregg, Rev. J. Milton Waldron, A.W. Price, A.L. Lewis, James H. Lewis, I.H. Burney, James H. Lewis II, and Gilyard Glover.

This new building for the home office of the Afro-American Life Insurance Company was dedicated on April 22, 1956. By the 1970s, the company began to suffer financial problems, and in 1988, it was assumed by Atlanta Life Insurance Company for $500,000.

Employees of the Cleveland M. Shaw Funeral Home at 915 East Union Street stand outside of the Shaw Building, which also housed at one time the Peoples Insurance Company. The officers for the insurance company were: Cleveland M. Shaw (president), Mrs. S.B. Shaw (vice-president), and Lillian Daughtey (secretary and treasurer).

James Edgar Whittington opened his funeral home in 1921. He was also one of the organizers and the first president of the Florida Negro Funeral Directors Association.

The medical building of Dr. Israel E. Williams was located at 102 E. Union Street. A West Indian by birth, he was a very successful physician, having served as the first African-American chief of staff for Methodist Hospital. Dr. Williams created the formula for Kramer Cough Syrup and also developed the formula for a tablet for heart patients. These products were sold by Reyno Pharmacy. He established the Velveteen Chemical Company, which developed formulas for hair preparations, such as a hair grower, hair restorer, hair shampoo, hair tonic, and conditioner.

Originally the site of the Davis Street Drug Store, Reyno Pharmacy (which is now demolished) was located at 630 Davis Street at the corner of Davis and Beaver Streets; it later moved to Davis and W. Ashley Streets. Lowe's Cut Rate Drug Store later operated at this location. Some of the early black pharmacists in the city were Dr.'s Earlinn Thompson, R.W. Butler, T.C. Christopher, R.E. Smith, W.C. Parrish, and R.C. Collins

Joseph and Rose Hackel were owners, along with others, of the Ritz Theater. The Ritz, opened in September 1929, was another theater for blacks in Jacksonville. Built by Neil Witschen, the theater was run by the Hackels for twenty-five years, until 1954 when it was sold to new management. The Hackels and their five daughters had come to Florida from Georgia and had been in the theater industry for many years. The Ritz closed in 1972.

African-American women worked as domestics in the home of many prominent white families in Jacksonville. Lola Pollock Harris, whose family resided on Davis and Louisiana Streets, worked for over twenty years for the Hackel family, which owned the Ritz Theater. This photograph was taken at Sandy's Studio on Broad Street in 1931.

Before psychics became fashionable, Professor Fleming (pictured in front of the Reyno Pharmacy) would appear around town, performing and lecturing on street corners.

Prospect Cleaners, pictured here *c.* 1948, was located at 607 Davis Street and was owned by Roscoe Jackson and his family.

Pictured here are African-American employees of Daylight Grocery Store. Daylight Grocery was one of the most successful chains of grocery stores in Jacksonville, with stores in several locations in the city.

The Davis Street Shoe Factory, c. 1949, was one of several shoe stores. On the eastside was Oscar Mathis Shoe Store.

The Central Metropolitan C.M.E. Church, founded in 1905, was located at 1079 Davis Street.

Huff Funeral Home on Davis Street was established in the 1920s by Andrew Huff. Mr. Huff died in 1946, and the business was assumed by two female employees. It is one of the oldest remaining businesses on Davis Street.

Members of the First New Mt. Zion Baptist Church, founded in 1921, break ground next to their old structure for the construction of their new church on Davis Street. The church was located across the street from the Darnell Cookman Junior High School.

Faculty members of the Davis Street Junior High School pose for this photograph. The school building was erected in 1947. Professor Anderson served as principal for many years. The original Davis Street School opened in the early 1920s.

This is a photograph of the Davis Street Junior High School basketball team, *c.* 1940.

The Sowell Funeral Home, established by Victoria Sowell, was located at 1439 Davis Street. She owned the Mt. Pleasant Cemetery, one of several African-American-owned cemeteries.

Three
Mr. Weems

"He was "The photographer" of Black Jacksonville"

Ellie Weems, a native of McDonough, Georgia, began his photography career in Atlanta on Auburn Avenue before moving in 1929 to Jacksonville, where he opened his first photography studio at Broad and Duval Streets. A few years later, he moved to W. Ashley Street.

This house on Beaver Street became Weems's third and final studio and was a landmark for over fifty years. He remained here until he became ill and his nephew George Rice moved him to Atlanta in 1981.

Mr. Weems photographed everything in Black Jacksonville from baby portraits to corpses, from street scenes to social events, and from school events to family portraits. Even though there were several other studios, like Sandy's on Broad Street and Artistic and Avery Studio on Davis Street, none obtained the same success of Mr. Weems. Today, thousands of his negatives are located at the Auburn Avenue Research Library in Atlanta, Georgia.

The Betsch family are, clockwise, from left to right: Mrs. Mary Lewis Betsch, Marvyne, Johnnetta, John T., and son John Thomas Jr., c. 1950s. John Betsch owned several businesses on Ashley Street and worked for Afro-American Life Insurance before his death in 1953; Mrs. Betsch taught at Edwards Waters College and was vice president at the Afro-American Life Insurance before her death in 1975; Marvyne, "the Mayor of American Beach," resides in Fernandina, Florida; Johnetta became the first African-American president of Spelman College; and John Jr. is a jazz drummer in Europe.

The Easter Parade of 1941 featured the Harris children: (from left to right) Catherine, Henry, and Deloris. Their house at 1410 Louisiana Street, the first on the left side of the then sandy street, was a hangout for many kids on the street. According to family lore, they had the first television on the block.

Professor A. St. George Richardson (shown with his wife Sarah and their sons A. St. George Jr. and Robert) had a distinguished career as an educator and businessman. A former president of Morris Brown College in Atlanta, Richardson was a cashier for the Anderson and Company Bank in the 1920s and was the deputy internal revenue collector and assistant secretary over the bookkeeping and accounting department for the Afro-American Life Insurance Company, c. 1943.

The Forrest children Jerome and Olivia, both named for their parents and pictured here c. 1930s, were two of four children of Jerome and Olivia Forrest, longtime residents of Louisiana Street. Mrs. Forrest, along with others, helped to organize the Louisiana Street reunion in 1981, a celebration of former residents of the street and surrounding areas in the Hogan Creek Community.

Mr. Weems would travel to homes to take family portraits, as he did with the Stuart Family who posed in their living room for this family portrait in 1950.

This is a *c.* 1940 photograph of Mrs. Iona Walker, daughter Priscilla (on right), and cousin Virginia Bouler (on left). The Walkers lived at 915 W. Monroe Street, where Brewster Hospital had its beginning. The Walkers also owned a cafe on Monroe Street. Not shown is Julious W. Walker, one of Jacksonville's most successful businessmen. Mr. Walker, a native of Georgia, came to Jacksonville in 1918 and opened a fish market on West Adams Street. In 1937, he acquired property on W. Monroe and operated a grocery store and fish market. During World War II, he employed eighteen people and served the public 24 hours a day. The Walker store was renamed Brown Cafe when daughter Priscilla and her husband Raiford acquired the property.

Patricia, Linda, and Ms. Geneva Howard (pictured from left to right) pose for this photograph, *c.* 1955. Pat and Linda were students at Northwestern High School and resided in the Magnolia Garden area on Lantana Avenue.

Japhus Baker, the nephew of Wyatt Geter, took over the funeral home opened by his uncle in 1895 and renamed it Geter and Baker. The home was located on Beaver Street (c. 1941). Baker was the first licensed embalmer in Florida. In 1973, Rev. Charles E. Toston became the owner and changed the name to Toston Funeral Home.

Mrs. Willie Manigault stands with four of her children who attended the Sunshine Day Nursery Kindergarten at 1124 W. Beaver Street. The nursery was a division of the Jacksonville Welfare League and the Community Chest.

Lawton L. Pratt opened his funeral home, picture here *c.* 1947, in 1900 at 525–527 W. Beaver Street. Pratt was one of the organizers of the Florida Negro Funeral Directors and Embalmers Association and worked to open the field of funeral service to women. Pratt's slogan was "The Funeral Home of the Community."

Oscar Hillman assumed ownership of the former Lawton Pratt Funeral Home.

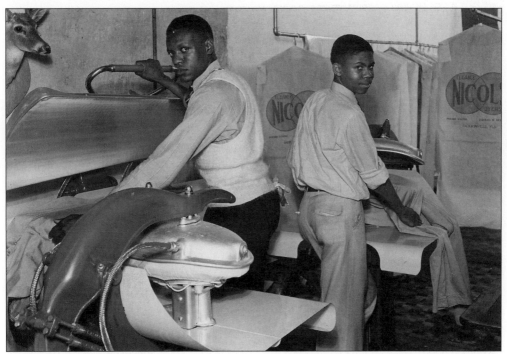

Two pressers at the Nichols Dry Cleaners on W. Beaver Street are shown here in this photograph. Other businesses once located on Beaver Street included the American Legion Post, Anderson Cleaners, and the office of Dr. Cassius Ward.

Members of the American Legion promote their national convention in front of the Broad and Beaver Skating Rink, *c.* 1948.

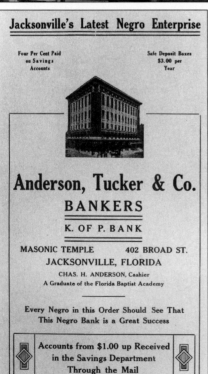

The Masonic Temple at Broad and Duval Streets was built in 1913 under the administration of Grand Master John H. Dickerson and paid for during the administration of Grand Master D.D. Powell. The construction for the $500,000, five-story, fireproof brick building began in 1912 and was completed in 1913. The building housed numerous businesses, including Pedro Mendez's Tailoring Shop, Anderson, Tucker & Co Bank, the law offices of Daniel W. Perkins, the Florida State Teachers Association, the *Jacksonville Journal*, and the NAACP.

This is an advertisement for the Anderson, Tucker & Co Bank. Another major business located on Broad (not pictured) was the popular Richmond Hotel, operated by Mrs. Alice Kirkpatrick. The 48-room hotel opened in 1909 and featured a tea room. It was the hotel of the stars who would visit Jacksonville, including Cab Calloway, Billie Holiday, and Ella Fitzgerald.

Standing in front of the Masonic Building are delegates to the National Negro Insurance Association who met in Jacksonville for its annual meeting on April 20–22, 1932. In the background is Pedro Mendez's Cuban Tailor Shop. Mendez, a native of Santiago, Cuba, moved to Jacksonville in 1925.

The Duval County 4-H Club stands under the canopy of the Masonic Building, c. 1934

Housed in the 400 block of Broad Street were several businesses. One of these businesses was the Jacksonville home office of the Atlanta Life Insurance Company, which occupied the top floor of the building. The storefronts, including the Reliable Shoe Store, Sandy's Photograph Studio, Starling and Son News Stand, and Sister's Beauty Shop, were all located at the corner of Broad and Duval Streets. For a very short time McGill and McGriff Law Offices were located in this building. (Note the poster advertising the movie *The Great Zigfield* playing at the Strand Theater.)

The Daysprings Baptist Church was located at 1043 Jefferson Street in the Hansontown area. This new structure was built in 1939 next to the original site (on the left). Jefferson Street was primarily residential and was the gateway to the Sugar Hill community.

One of the most popular spots for kids during the hot summer days was the Jefferson Street Pool. It was located at Jefferson and Fourth Streets, c. 1948. Other "swimming holes" were Gillis Lake and Moncrief Creek. Shown above is a baptism ceremony that often took place at the pool.

The home of Dr. Warren J. Schell was originally owned by Dr. Carey V. Freeman, a dentist. Dr. Schell practiced medicine for many years and was very active in the community, serving as chairman of the Jacksonville Urban League.

Brewster Hospital began serving the Jacksonville community in 1885. It was located in a Queen Anne-style home on Monroe Street until 1901, when it was sold to the Women's Missionary Society of the Methodist Church. Mrs. George A. Brewster donated $1,500 to the Missionary Society to establish the hospital and nurse training program. Local author B.J. Sessions has documented the history of Brewster Hospital in her book A *Charge to Keep: 1901–1966.*

The leading physicians from the state of Florida, pictured here in *c.* 1940s, attended seminars at Brewster Hospital. Seminars were conducted in Tuberculosis, Venereal Disease, and Pediatrics.

Four
Events

Mrs. Booker T. Washington (center), national president of the Colored Women's Club, visited Jacksonville at the invitation of the Eartha M.M. White (far right) and the Colored Women's Club in 1913, two years before the death of her husband, who was president of Tuskegee University. Her visit included an appearance at Bethel Baptist Institute and the Old Folks Home. (University of North Florida Archives.)

Women's Mass Meeting

Where Men Are Invited

Non-Partisan Registration Meeting

TO BE HELD IN

Pythian Temple

August 20th

At 8 O'clock

The whole family is invited to hear why Negroes should register now! Come and hear for yourself!

Registration books open at county building, Monday, Tuesday and Wednesday

MISS E. M. M. WHITE, chairman

This is an announcement of the Women's Mass Meeting at the Knights of Pythian Temple, date unknown. (University of North Florida Archives.)

The A.G. Allen Minstrel Performers rally outside of the Royal Hotel, announcing their upcoming performance, c. 1920s. (University of North Florida Archives.)

The Elite Circle and Girls DeLuxe Club

expect you and your friends to enjoy

'An Aerial Frolic"

honoring

Miss Bessie Coleman

May 1, 8:30 to 12 P. M.   Pythian Auditorium

Subscription 75c

Music by the Imperial Jazz Orchestra

This is the invitation announcing the appearance of aviatrix Bessie Coleman in Jacksonville. Her visit to the city would result in her tragic death during an aerial performance on April 30, 1926, when her plane crashed during a practice run at Paxon Field. A memorial service was held at Bethel Church before her body was transported to Chicago. (University of North Florida Archives.)

The St. Paul Girl Scout Troop 293 and Brownie Troop 261 pose for this picture, c. 1945. At one time, a day camp for the girl scouts was held during the summer at the Emmanuel Episcopal Church grounds in South Jacksonville. Some of the other early girl scout troops were Troop 8, located at Second Baptist Church, and Troop 249, located at Mt. Ararat Baptist Church.

These boy scouts attended the boy scout camp at Camp Berlin on the St. John's River (now known as Dames Point). They were a part of several local boy scout troops in the city organized by boy scout pioneer David Dwight. Troop 51 was first organized in 1926 at Stanton High School. Other troops would be established by the Suwannee District at Mt. Zion, St. Pius, St. Stevens, and Bethel Churches by 1930.

When World War II hit this country, Josephus Pollock was one of thousands of African-American men in Jacksonville who were drafted or enlisted to fight for their country, c. 1942. African-American families received war ration stamps, and USO Clubs were set up in several locations. Many African Americans worked at the Jacksonville Naval Air Station and Camp Blanding.

The annual Afro-American Baby Contest, shown here c. 1940s, was a greatly anticipated event in Jacksonville.

Ethel Davenport, a well-known gospel singer, electrifies the audience at the annual Gospel Train program, c. 1940s. Musical guests included some of the nation's top and local acts.

A big event of the social season was the Omega Psi Phi Fraternity "Que Ca Pade" dance. Stanton student Viola Kittles (center) was named "Omega Sweetheart." Members of the Stanton High School majorette squad, dressed in sailor suits, performed during the dance, c. 1950.

Janie Mason, a longtime employee of Lily's Drug Store, was named A.L. Lewis "Mother of the Year." She participated in the annual school's homecoming parade where her daughter Joann attended school, *c*. 1959.

The wedding of Olivia "Pat" Forrest and David E. Parker was a glorious event held at Bethel Baptist Institute, *c*. 1950. From left to right are: bridesmaids Rosa Lee, two unidentified women, Olive Forrest (bride), Lorretta Golden, and Deloris Harris. The groomsmen, from left to right, are: unidentified, Jerome Forrest, David Parker (groom), Jimmy ?, John Lewis, and ? Parker.

55

Mother Midway Church on Van Buren was established in 1865 as the first African Methodist Episcopal church in Florida. It was founded by an ex-slave, William Stewart, and sixteen other men after the Confederate surrender in Florida. The church was named "Midway" from the name of a settlement between Jacksonville and New Berlin. The first church was housed east of 8th Street from 1875 to 1879. In 1921, the church moved to Van Buren, pictured *c.* 1945.

This is a *c.* 1941 photograph of the Mt. Calvary Baptist Church Choir. The church, established in 1892, was located at 301 Spruce Street in the old Brooklyn/Riverside neighborhood.

56

Five

Churches

The West Friendship Baptist Church on Carrie Street is picture here *c.* 1938.

Zion Hope Baptist Church on W. Church Street was established in 1929.

The Mount Zion A.M.E. Church at 201 E. Beaver Street was founded in 1866. This Romanesque structure was built after the fire of 1901.

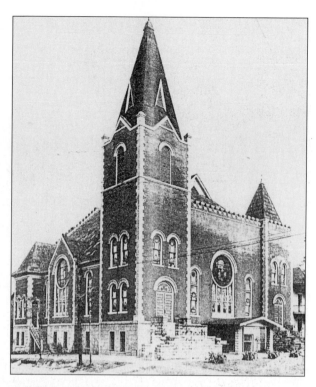

Second Baptist Church was organized in 1849 by Rev. Mack Brown. Rev. King David Britt (on the left) began pastoring the Second Baptist on Kings Road in 1929. Born in 1886 in Marianna, Florida, Rev. Britt also served as chairman of the Trustee Board for Florida Memorial College. He is shown with members of the Usher Board (1936).

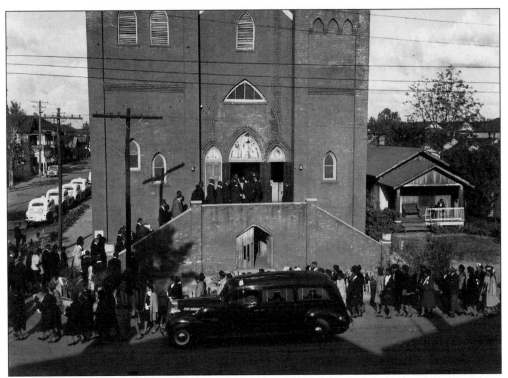

Shiloh Baptist Church was established in 1875. Shortly afterwards, Rev. James Johnson, father of James Weldon Johnson, pastored the church from the 1880s to 1901. The church was constructed on Logan Street.

Rev. Cleveland M. Shaw and the congregation of Shaw Baptist Church Baptist Church choir prepare to record an album, c. 1950s.

Rev. Dallas Graham and members of Mt. Ararat Baptist, pictured c. 1938, stand in front of the original church on the corner of Davis and 21st Streets. Rev. Graham was an outspoken advocate for equal pay and voting rights in Jacksonville. He challenged the Democratic party's "white-only" primary, and he won in 1945 after the circuit court ruled in his favor.

The second structure of Mt. Ararat was located on Myrtle and 21st Streets, c. 1940. In 1944, the church purchased property and built a sanitarium on Davis and 20th Streets, and in 1952, they opened a convalescent home. Rev. Graham pastored Mt. Ararat from 1926–1976.

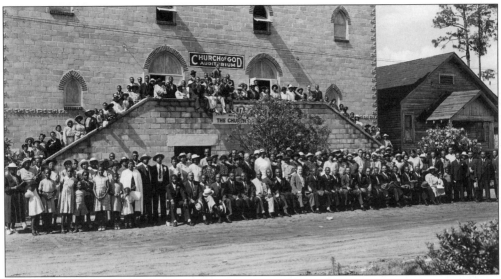

This is a *c.* 1940 photograph of the Church of God Auditorium at Steele and Blue Streets, founded in 1921.

The Central Baptist Church was located 115 W. State Street, pictured *c.* 1930s.

The Ebenezer M.E. Church at 432 West Ashley Street and Clay Street was founded as the Zion Methodist Episcopal Church in 1864. In 1881, the church was renamed Ebenezer.

The Emmanuel Baptist Church was located on Chelsea Avenue, *c.* 1949.

The Sunday school department stands in front of historic Bethel Baptist Institutional Church on Hogan Street in the Springfield community. It is the oldest church in Jacksonville for African Americans. It was founded in 1838 by four whites and two blacks under the leadership

of Rev. James McDonald. The first church was destroyed in the fire in 1901, and the church was rebuilt in 1904.

The West Union Baptist Church, located on Acorn Street, was organized in 1900. It is pictured here *c.* 1940s.

The Tabernacle Institutional Baptist Church, located on Albert and LaFayette Streets, was established in 1893. This photograph was taken *c.* 1943.

Simpson Memorial Tabernacle, pictured here *c.* 1947 on the corner of Kings Road and Cleveland Street, was established in 1884. This structure was erected in 1923, and it burned in 1942. During the 1920s, the church had an athletic association, a literary club, and a music and trade school. It is now known as Simpson United Methodist Episcopal Church.

There were numerous African-American-owned cemeteries in Jacksonville, including Duval, Greenwood, Memorial, Mt. Olive Memorial Park, Mt. Pleasant, Old City, and Sunset Cemetery. Several were owned by the Afro-American Life Insurance Company.

S.A. "Buddy" Austin was a local vaudeville comedian who produced shows in Jacksonville during the 1920s and 1930s. In 1921, he starred in several silent movies produced by Norman Studios in Jacksonville, including *The Green Eye Monster*. Norman's Studio also produced Bill Pickett's *The Bull Dogger* in 1922. Later in his life, Austin owned the Strand Theater for a period of time and worked in the department of public relations for Afro-American Life Insurance Company.

Six

Entertainment

"We remember the lights coming on in the theater and then Miss Emma Lee Turner and Leroy Jackson checking the cut list while Prof. Anderson waited outside. We run but couldn't hide.

"Jay Jay" in the Chips off the Block Column
Florida Star Newspaper, Nov. 9, 1957

The cast of Irvin Miller's Brown Skin Revue appears here on the stage of the Strand Theater, *c.* 1940s. Other popular theaters for blacks were the Frolic, opened in 1913; the Roosevelt, opened in 1949; the Ritz Theater, opened in 1929; and the Pixie Theater on the Eastside, which featured live acts and shows.

Jacksonville had many local entertainers like Happy Reid who performed throughout the city during the 1930s and 1940s.

Ray Charles Robinson left St. Augustine's School for the Deaf and Blind around 1945 and moved to Jacksonville where he lived with his aunt on Church Street. He hung out at Lenape's Tavern with other musicians looking for work. He had a short stint with the big band of Henry Washington and played occasionally at the Two Spot Night Club. Charles also played with the Tiny York Combo. It was Tiny who helped Charles leave Jacksonville, where he dropped his last name to avoid confusion with the boxer and rose to fame as Ray Charles.

James "Charlie Edd" Craddock, seen here c. 1951, was one of the wealthiest and most prosperous businessmen in Jacksonville. He owned several businesses, including the Charlie Edd Hotel, the Blue Chip Hotel, Young Men's Smoke Shop, a Pawn Shop, and the Two Spot Nite Club. He died in 1957.

On Christmas Day in 1940, James "Charlie Edd" Craddock opened the Two Spot Club at 45th Street and Moncrief. The hardwood oak floors could accommodate two thousand people and another thousand could be seated on the main floor and mezzanine, which ran around three sides. There were several private dining rooms in the air-conditioned facility with a cafeteria and a bar. The club, seen here c. 1941, was sold after his death and renamed the Palms Ballroom in 1957.

Two jitterbugs swing at a dance at the Two Spot. It was the hottest club in Jacksonville and featured headline acts such as Dinah Washington, Sam Cooke, Jackie Wilson, James Brown, Lionel Hampton, and Ruth Brown.

The Afro-American Life Insurance Company's annual dance, seen here *c*. 1950s, at the Two Spot Club was one of the anticipated social events of the season.

Nat Small, a trumpet player, was the band leader of the combo Nat Small and the Small Nats. It was one of the many bands that played at the Two Spot Club. Others included "Skeet" Hampton, Henry Washington, Teddy Washington and Baron J. McCloud, Tiny York, and Alonzo Ross.

Most fraternities, sororities, and clubs held their annual dances and balls at the Two Spot, including members of the Kappa Alpha Psi, whose court is shown at a dance in 1951.

Mr. Weems photographed this unidentified band in his studio during the 1930s. Many of the bands played in the Knights of Pythias Hall, the Elks Club, and the live shows at the local theaters, such as the Frolic and the Roosevelt.

The USO Club at Wilder Park in the Federal Recreation Building, which was operated by the National Catholic Community Service Organization, was a site for social events and dances.

World War II soldiers and their guests relax and enjoy games at the USO Club. This inset in this picture is Mrs. Eartha M.M. White.

The Roxy Social Club Anniversary dance featured the Baron McCloud Clouds of Joy band and vocalist, c. 1941.

The Norfolk Singers, later renamed the Sons of Jubilee Singers, were one of the city's most popular male groups. They performed a radio broadcast for WMBR.

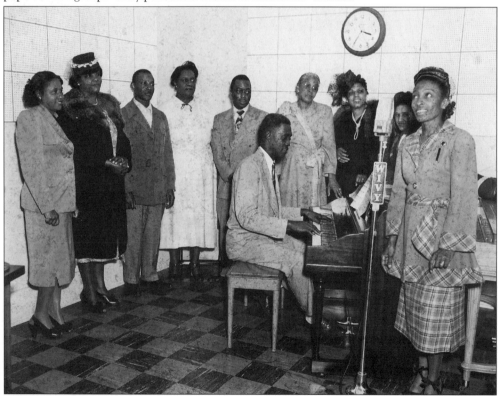

Ethel Davenport and an unidentified group perform over the waves of radio WIVY, c. 1949.

Cecil Limbric was a popular radio personality during the 1940s. Cecil was the grandson of the Rev. Zacharia Limbrick, owner of several barbershops in the city. One of the other radio disc jockeys was Ken Knight, who began his work in Jacksonville at WRHC and hosted the popular "Sweet Chariot" program and the Pepsi Teen hour at the Roosevelt Theater.

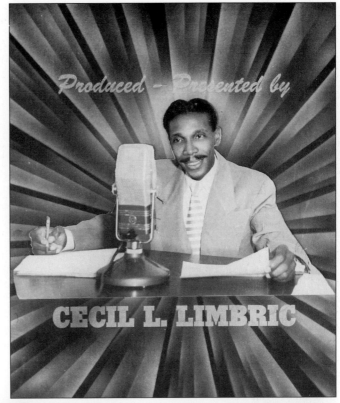

This is a photograph of pianist and musician John Bustamante, *c.* 1940s.

Jacksonville native and Eastside resident Billy Daniels went on to become a national singing star when he sang "That Old Black Magic" at the Club Harlem in 1942. The recording of the song sold over 12 million copies. When he was a child, his family did not even realize that Billy could sing until he sang one Sunday morning at St. Phillips Episcopal Church. During his career, he recorded many albums. His daughter Yvonne was a popular disc jockey at WOBS Radio Station in the 1950s. Billy Daniels died in 1988 and is buried Los Angeles.

While the Two Spot was the place for dancing, the Duval County Armory hosted larger shows with artists such as Louis Jordan, Duke Ellington, Count Basie, and Cab Calloway. Above is "The Big Show of 1951" at the Armory which featured Nat King Cole and Sarah "Sassy" Vaughn.

Seven

Homes

This is one of the fine homes on W. Monroe Street in the Lavilla Park area, c. 1930s. Lavilla was one of the oldest communities for African Americans in Jacksonville.

This *c.* 1941 photograph shows the home of Bishop Henry Young Tookes, a 1914 graduate of Edward Waters College. Elected in 1932, he was the third Florida native to serve as bishop of the African Methodist Episcopal Church. Under his administration, Edward Waters College was accredited and a library was erected. His house was built in 1939 at 1011 West Eighth Street and was a part of the fashionable "Sugar Hill" section. It is now used as the AKA Sorority House. Bishop Tookes died in 1948.

This is the home of Bishop George Edward Curry. He was elected the sixtieth bishop of the A.M.E. Church in 1940 and was also a graduate of both Morris Brown College and Edward Waters College.

The Blodgett Homes, the third public housing project in the city, was constructed in 1942 and named in honor of Joseph Haygood Blodgett, a wealthy building contractor and developer who died in 1934. It opened with 654 units and cleared the Hansontown slum area north of State Street. It was developed on 53 acres of land, and rent ranged between $12 and $43. John Simms, former manager of Durkeeville, managed the projects. It was demolished in 1993.

This is an unidentified birthday party in Blodgett Homes, 1952.

This is a view of the Durkeeville Housing Project which opened in 1937 as the first housing project for African Americans in Jacksonville. It was followed by the construction of the

Brentwood and then Blodgett Homes.

The owner of the Prospect Cleaners and his family pose in front of their home on Davis Street.

The houses in the "Sugar Hill" community, located at 8th and Jefferson Streets near Springfield and now occupied by the medical center, were the homes of some of Jacksonville's most affluent African Americans, like A.L. Lewis, Afro-American Insurance founder; William Raines, educator; and Isaiah and Sara Blocker, to name just a few. The entire area was demolished for the growth and development of the medical facilities and hospitals.

Eight

Outings

"Cars galore and yellow buses line the narrow streets
Hailing from Brunswick, Savannah and Jacksonville
Filled to capacity and then they unload the coolers and large tin tubs . . .
Nights away doing the Hully Gully, slow drag and the swing"

Ruth Ann Lunah Waters, c. 1960.

African Americans enjoy an outing at Manhattan Beach, a resort located 20 miles from Jacksonville, c. 1926. The beach was operated by a group of successful African-American businessmen, including S.A. "Buddy" Austin, owner of the Strand Theater; B.C. Vanderhorst; Japhus Baker; D.D. Powell; and William Schenck, a local business owner who also owned a barber shop and pool room on Broad Street.

This is a photograph of the Hotel Manhattan and Board Walk on Manhattan Beach, *c.* 1920. The owners of the beach offered a thousand shares to the general public at 12.50 per share. Shareholders also came from Georgia.

Bathing beauties pose inside of the beach house on Manhattan Beach, *c.* 1930.

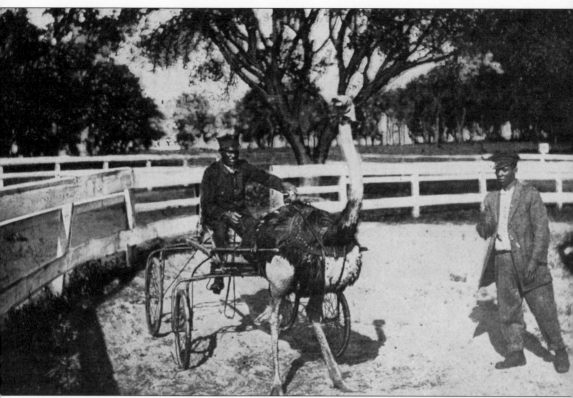

Florida offered numerous ostrich farms where families would go for a pleasurable afternoon. Jacksonville's first ostrich farm was located out Tallyerand Avenue in the Fairfield section east of downtown. It opened in the winter of 1898. Visitors could watch ostrich races and ride in ostrich-drawn carts. Later, a zoo component was added and it included alligators and baby lions. By 1907, air balloons, parachute jumps, comedy acrobats, high-wire acts, free vaudeville acts, roller coasters, and merry-go-rounds could be found at the farm. Admission was 10¢.

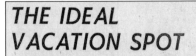

This is an American Beach advertisement which appeared in the *Pittsburgh Courier*. The beach was established by A.L. Lewis and the Afro-American Life Insurance Company through Pension Bureau Funds. They purchased 33 acres of land with oceanfront view from the estate of Richard Delafield and later added over 180 acres to develop American Beach in Fernandina, Florida.

This is one of the several homes owned by Afro-American employees on American Beach near Amelia Island and Fernandina Beach, Florida. The streets were named for Afro-American founders. Hotels included the A. Lewis Motel, the Blue Palace, Lee's Ocean Vu Inn, and Martha Hippard's Hideaway.

Annually, Eartha White would host summer outings with bands and music at the 18-acre site of the old Moncrief Springs, which she acquired in 1945. The original site had been developed as early as 1874.

The Clara White Mission had the pool renovated, and the Moncrief Springs became a recreation center where children played. In its early years, there was also a horse-race track.

Two giants in the cause of humanity, Jacksonville's "Angel of Mercy" Eartha M.M. White (left) and Mary McLeod Bethune, stand on W. Ashley Street. Eartha White had worked to care for the sick and wounded during the Spanish-American War in 1898. She died in 1974. Her friend, the indomitable Mary McLeod Bethune, was the founder of Bethune Cookman College and the National Council of Negro Women. Mrs. Bethune was a frequent visitor to Jacksonville.

Mrs. Margaret Sims worked with the American Red Cross roll call pledges and was a well-known singer and civic worker in Jacksonville.

Nine
Pioneers/Work

African Americans migrated to Jacksonville from Georgia, South Carolina, and Alabama from 1866 to the 1920s. One of these many families was the Howard family, who settled in the area at the turn of the century.

The National Hall Building housed the Freedman's Bank during the 1870s and 1880s. The bank was created to assist ex-slaves.

Jonathan C. Gibbs (1847–1874) was the first African American appointed as secretary of the state of Florida. On November 8, 1868, he was elected as a delegate to the Florida Constitutional Convention and was vice president of the Jacksonville Republican Convention.

George E. Ross (pictured to the right) was one of five African Americans elected to the Jacksonville City Council in 1887 after the City's charter expanded the boundaries to include black neighborhoods. Other members included Rev. Capers M. Vaught, pastor of St. John's Baptist Church; J. Douglas Wetmore, attorney; John R. Scott; and C.C. Manigault. These men were instrumental in helping blacks in Jacksonville recover from the devastation of the fire of 1901.

Joseph E. Lee was a former municipal judge of Jacksonville, Florida, from 1887 to 1889; collector of customs from 1890 to 1894 and from 1897 to 1898; and collector of internal revenue from 1898 to 1913.

The Rev. Dr. J. Milton Waldron, pastor of Bethel Baptist Institutional Church, was born in Lynchburg, Virginia, in 1863 and educated at Lincoln University and Newton Theological Seminary. After fifteen years in Jacksonville, Waldron moved to Washington, D.C. and pastored the Shiloh Baptist Church. He died in 1931.

Mrs. M.E. Smith was the first African-American club woman in Florida. She organized the M.E. Smith Club for African-American women. After the fire of 1901, she fed and housed twenty people in her home.

Father Henry Harrison, born in 1810 in Nassau County, arrived in Jacksonville when it was called Cowford. He played with Native American children and learned their language. Harrison was also a preacher and preached for eighty-nine years. He named Eartha M.M. White three months before she was born. He died at the age of 107 in 1917. (University of North Florida Archive.)

Squire English, an early Jacksonville pioneer, owned the property on Ashley Street where the Clara White Mission is located. He sold the property around 1912 to Charles Crowd, who built the Globe Theater on that spot. (University of North Florida Archives.)

Abraham Lincoln Lewis was born March 28, 1864, in Marianna (Madison County), Florida. He moved to Jacksonville in 1876 and received his education. He founded the Afro-American Life Insurance Company, the Lincoln Golf and Country Club, and American Beach; Lewis was the most successful business- and civic-minded leader in Jacksonville. The Lavilla School was renamed in his honor. He resided with his family in the "Sugar Hill" section on 8th Street until his death in 1947.

The Wilder Park Branch Library was the only library for African Americans in Jacksonville. The first library opened in 1927. Some of the pioneer librarians were Mrs. Lofton, Mrs. Arabella DeCoursey, Mrs. Jenerette, and Mrs. Olga Owens Bradham.

The ice and fuel wagon was a familiar site in the African-American neighborhoods in Jacksonville. They went from neighborhood to neighborhood selling blocks of ice, bundles of firewood, and coal.

The Law Library of Attorney Simuel D. McGill is pictured here c. 1941. Simuel D. McGill, a 1902 graduate of Edward Waters College, worked as a part-time law clerk in the offices of James Weldon Johnson and was admitted to the Florida Bar in 1908 after having completed his law training at Boston University. McGill successfully argued one of the most historic cases in Florida involving Abe Washington, who was spared from hanging and the electric chair in 1925. After a successful career, McGill died on March 15, 1951.

Raiford Brown (second barber from left) and other barbers pose for this photograph in the Crowd's Barbershop on East Bay Street. The shop served Jacksonville's professional white clientele only. Raiford Brown moved to Jacksonville from Georgetown, South Carolina, and resided on the east side of Jacksonville. He helped to secure library services for his community, and today, a library bears his name.

These are African-American employees at the George Washington Hotel, located downtown on Adams and Julia Streets, c. 1930s. The George Washington Hotel was one of the finest hotels in Jacksonville.

Ten

Clubs

Black Jacksonville had hundreds of social clubs, like the Owl Club. The club's officers are pictured here *c.* 1930s.

These are members of the Porters Association, *c.* 1930s. A. Phillip Randolph organized the Brotherhood of Sleeping Car Porters. He grew up in Jacksonville and attended Cookman Institute on Davis Street. His father Rev. James Randolph founded what is now the New Hope A.M.E Church.

This is a 1942 photograph of the fiftieth anniversary of the Bricklayers Union No. 2, which was chartered in 1892.

The Excelsior Ladies Saving Club holds their annual dance at the Two Spot Club in 1948.

The heart and soul of civic and social development for blacks in Jacksonville assemble on the steps of Stanton High School, c. 1940s. They are, from left to right: (front row) L.M. Argrett, W.H. Lee, Lawton Pratt, Boyd, A.B. Coleman, Joe H. James, and Daniel Perkins; (second row) Joe Higdon, J.I.E. Scott, S.A. Austin, Dr. A.W. Smith, and B.C. Vanderhost; (third row) William Robinson, Ralph Lee, Ed Vaughn, R.T. Thomas, and Dr. W.L. Redmond; (fourth row) Porsher Taylor, Ed Rodriquez, Al Joyner, Dr. I.E. Williams, and unidentified; (fifth row) Dr. Waters, Joe McLane, Dr. Flipper, and unidentified. (University of North Florida Archives.)

In 1869, the Stanton Normal School was dedicated and named in honor of General Edwin M. Stanton, an outspoken abolitionist and secretary of war under President Abraham Lincoln. Stanton High School is shown before the fire on May 1, 1901. In 1894, James Weldon Johnson became principal and served for eight years. Notable students included T. Thomas Fortune, a journalist, and J. Rosamond Johnson, composer and musician.

This is a picture of the rebuilt Stanton High School after it was destroyed by fire in 1901.

Eleven

Schools

"God preserve our love for Stanton
God preserve her light
May our precepts learned of Stanton, guide us ever right . . ."

Stanton High Alma Mater

The third Stanton High School was constructed in 1915 on the original site and was completed in 1917. The African-American principals were James C. Waters, Daniel W. Culp, William M. Artrell, James Weldon Johnson, Simon P. Robinson, Isaiah A. Blocker, George M. Sampson, James N. Wilson, Floyd J. Anderson, Jessie L. Terry, Charles D. Brooks, and Benjamin Durham Jr. In 1953, the new Stanton High School opened on 13th Street, and this building later closed in 1971.

The 1932 girls basketball team for Stanton High School poses for this group picture.

The Stanton High School Marching Blue Devils Band marches by the school during one of the many parades it participated in annually.

A 1951 nighttime game at Durkee Stadium features the high-stepping majorettes, under the direction of Mrs. E.L. George, and the Stanton High School Marching Blue Devils Band, under the direction of Mr. K.D. McFarlin. The drum major was Bertram Wilson and the majorettes were Virginia Singleton, Deloris Harris, Veola Kittles, Deloris Muldrow, and Offie Osborne.

This is the Stanton High School basketball team, *c.* 1941

Miss Stanton High School and her attendants are pictured here in their decorated car during the homecoming festivities, *c.* 1946.

Miss Edward Waters College is surrounded by her attendants and the cheerleaders, *c.* 1930s. The school's football team mascot was a tiger.

Edward Waters College, founded in 1891, was named for the third bishop of the A.M.E. Church, who was elected bishop in 1836. Bishop Edward Waters died in 1847 after a carriage accident. The B.F. Lee Seminary Building, a four-story brick building, was completed in 1925. The building housed the administrative offices of the theological department.

Built for $30,000 in 1916, Centennial Hall of Edward Waters College was named to commemorate the one-hundredth anniversary of the A.M.E. Church. It was designed by African-American architect and Jacksonville resident Rev. Richard L. Brown. The building currently houses the library for the school. It was built under the administration of Rev. John A. Gregg, who served from 1913 to 1920 as president. He was elected bishop in 1824.

107

Two graduates from the Class of 1907 of the Florida Baptist Academy are pictured with the principal Nathan W. Collier (center). The Florida Baptist Academy began in 1892 at Bethel Institutional Church under the pastorate of Rev. Matthew Gilbert. Born in South Carolina in 1862, Rev. Gilbert was a graduate of Colgate University and Union Theological Seminary. He died in 1917. (University of North Florida Archives.)

Members of the administration and faculty of the Boylan-Haven Boarding School, *c.* 1945, stand on the steps of the school founded to educate black girls. Moved to Franklin and Jessie Streets by 1910, the school was established in 1885 at Davis and Duval Streets as the Boylan Industrial Training School for Girls. Harriet E. Emerson named the school for Mrs. Ann Boylan Degroot of Newark, New Jersey, a former teacher of the Cookman School who gave the initial $1,000 for the school. In 1932, it merged with the Haven School of Savannah and the name was changed. It was under the auspices of the Women's Home Missionary Society Methodist Episcopal Church.

This is the Duval County Negro Vocational School.

Preschool education was taught at schools such as the Hope Day Nursery Kindergarten, which was under the auspices of the Association of Day Nurseries and affiliated with the Jacksonville Negro Welfare League of the Community Chest.

The Beaumont School of Nursing was located on West Beaver Street, c. 1950.

Students at the A.L. Lewis Junior High School in the Lavilla area prepare Thanksgiving baskets, *c*. 1951. The school was originally named the Lavilla High School.

St. Pius Catholic School was located on the corner of Lee and State Streets near the Ritz Theater, *c*. 1938.

Harlem Renaissance author and former Jacksonville resident Zora Neale Hurston poses with students performing a play on her book *Their Eyes Were Watching God, c. 1938.*

The homecoming court of Matthew W. Gilbert High School, located on the Eastside of Jacksonville, are pictured on the field during the halftime of their homecoming game. In 1938, William M. Raines served as principal of the school until his death in 1950. He was succeeded by Eugene Butler. Both former principals have schools named after them.

Twelve

Sports

In 1926, Durkee Stadium was constructed. It was named for Dr. J.H. Durkee, a doctor who owned the land at the corner of Eight and Myrtle Avenue. It was originally known as Barrs Field until the City's Department of Recreation acquired it. In 1980, the park was renamed the James P. "Bubbling" Smalls Park in memory of the longtime coach at Stanton High School. Coach Smalls, a 1928 graduate of Stanton High School, began coaching in 1934 and coached for thirty-four years. He retired with a record of 197–84–25 and nine city football championships.

One of the most popular teams in the Negro Southern League was the Jacksonville Red Caps, who played at Durkee Stadium. Owned by J.B. Greer, the Red Caps were, from left to right: (kneeling) Barnhill, Philip Homes, Flute Mitchell, and Ferrel; (standing) Howard "Duke" Cleveland, Joe Roal, David ?, Preacher Henry "Dad" Turner, Lacy Thomas, and Mint Jones; (behind the players) Cox. The picture was taken in front of the Terminal Station. Other players not pictured included Willie (Baby) Ray, Parnell "Red" Woods, and Herman Bell.

The Jacksonville Eagles baseball team was managed by "Big" Jim Williams. Many people played on the team, like Trickshot Washington, Peanut Davis, Lux Houston, Felix McLaurin, Jesse Blackman, Lefty McMillan, Charlie Harris, Horace Latham, Carswell, Greene, Blackman and Lefty Coleman, and Smitty Smith.

114

Leroy "Spike" Washington, a former player for the Jacksonville Giants, was the sports editor for the *Jacksonville Journal* and worked for the Afro-American Life Insurance Company in the division of publicity and public relations.

The Harlem Pharmacy team, pictured here c. 1942, was one of many business-sponsored baseball teams in the city.

The Roosevelt Department baseball team, *c*. 1948, was another one of these sponsored teams.

William "Bill" Lucas, shown in his 1953 senior picture from Stanton High School, had a successful career as a baseball player in the California League. After a stint in the the Army, he joined the Milwaukee Braves. In the 1970s, he became the manager of the Atlanta Braves baseball team, becoming one of the first of his race to be named to such a position. He died in 1978.

The Lincoln Golf and Country Club opened on May 21, 1927. Established by A.L. Lewis, the club was located at U.S. 1 and Richardson Road on acreage now covered by the Lincoln Estates and Carver Manor subdivisions. It closed in 1947. Golfing advocate Jimmy Burris reopened it in 1948 and operated it until 1953.

Many African-American men worked as caddies and locker-room attendants in the clubhouse at San Jose Golf Club.

Joe Louis, former Heavyweight Boxing Champion and an avid golfer, was a regular visitor to the 54-hole Lincoln Golf and Country Club. He accepted his first invitation to play in 1948. Golf champions were awarded the Sylvanus S. Hart trophy each year. Hart, a contractor and tax collector, was also one of Jacksonville's first black bankers. In 1947, Gertrude Styles organized the Ladies of the Link Golf Circle.

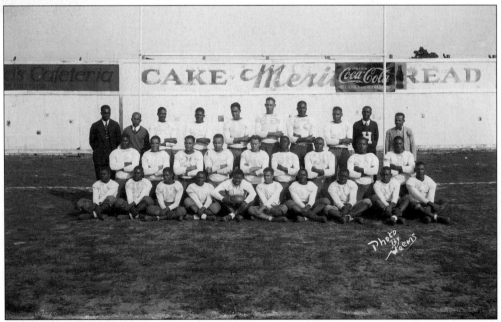

This is an unidentified football team, *c* . 1930s.

Thirteen
Outreach

*"Do all the good you can, In all the ways you can,
In all the places you can, For all the people you can,
While you can."*
Clara White

The Old Folks Home on Milnor Avenue was a division of the Community Chest. The Community Chest was organized in 1924 to afford the public an opportunity to contribute to such charitable organizations. The Jacksonville Negro Welfare Group was incorporated under the laws of Florida in 1925 as a non-profit organization and admitted to the Community Chest in 1926.

During the Great Depression of the late 1920s and early 1930s, Joe James administered relief food and clothing as the director of the Jacksonville Welfare League. James, a graduate of Clark College in Atlanta, was active in politics and was one of the founders of the Emancipation Day Celebration. He died in 1966.

The Recreation Center Building on Duval Street was constructed in 1914 and originally housed the Young Men's Hebrew Association because there was for a time a large Jewish population which resided in the area. After the end of World War I, the Maceo Elks Lodge took over the building, seen here c. 1938.

In 1925, the Jacksonville Welfare League established the Travelers Aid in Union Station's "colored" waiting room and offered assistance and relief to traveling passengers, c. 1939. The Union Station is now the Prime Osborn Convention Center.

The USO Service Club at Mt. Herman and Third Streets is shown here c. 1943.

These distinguished gentlemen are: John A. Broadnax (upper left); James Whittington (upper right); Robert Peppers (lower left); and Theodore Redding (lower right). Pictured on the opposite page are Joseph Higdon (left) and Dr. William L. Redmond (right).

On October 16, 1930, at the home of John A. Ross, the FlaJax Club, Inc. was organized. Pictured on these two pages are six of the eleven charter members; not shown are John Ross, Leroy Baker, A. St. George Richardson, Payton Roberts, and John Sims. It has stood for what is good for the communities it serves in Jacksonville and the state of Florida. The FlaJax Club, Inc. is primarily a civic and social organization made up of professional men from Jacksonville, Palatka, Gainesville, and other surrounding cities. The founding/charter members saw fit to organize young men and to cultivate an organization to express their needs for social, economic, and charitable endeavors for the black citizenry of Duval County and surrounding areas.

The Upsilon Lambda Chapter of Alpha Phi Alpha fraternity was established on September 15, 1926, by T.E. Morris, R.W. Butler, R.P. Crawford, A. St. George Richardson, L.A. McGee, Rudolph Gordon, and Robert Lynon. Here, members pose at their annual banquet in 1957.

The Gamma Rho Omega Chapter of Alpha Kappa Alpha sorority was chartered June 23, 1942. The chapter's charter members were Daisy Brookins, Edna Calhoun, Vivian Ingram, Elizabeth Jasmin, Louise Sheffield, Melba Sunday, Thelma Harris, Aldonia Seabrook, Helen Taylor, Coatsie Jones, Lois Roberts, Hattie McKissick, and Mildred White. From this chapter comes Supreme Basileus (*basileus* is Greek for president) Norma Ruth Solomon, a native of Jacksonville and graduate of Stanton High School.

Seen in this c. 1951 photograph, the Jacksonville Alumnae Chapter of Delta Sigma Theta, formerly known as Alpha Iota Sigma Chapter, was established in 1913 and included Winona Cargile Alexander (seated on the sofa, third from left), one of the founders of the national sorority at Howard University. Other charter members were Thelma Harris Livingston, Florida Rutledge, Cave, Willie Lee Joyner Lucas, Fay Glover Solomon, Lille Belle McKeever Blackshear, Mozelle Cornelia Bruton, Ali Thorpe, and Hazel Wiles Overstreet. Founding member Alexander died in 1984 at the age of 96.

The Kappa Alpha Psi brothers serenade at their dance at the Two Spot Night Club. The Jacksonville Alumni Chapter was organized on February 26, 1925 by Japhus Baker, Lemuel Bolton, and others.

The Theta Phi Chapter of Omega Psi Phi was chartered in 1925. The members sing their hymn at their annual dance at the Two Spot Night Club, c. 1950.

The Nu Beta Sigma Chapter of the Phi Beta Sigma fraternity was established on November 1, 1929. In this group picture, taken in 1947, is founder Leonard F. Morse, former president of Edward Waters College. He also founded in 1915 the Inter-Fraternal Council, later changed to the Pan Hellenic Council. He died on May 13, 1961.

Members of Zeta Phi Beta surround pianist Hazel Scott following a concert at the Roosevelt Theater in 1950. The charter members of the Beta Alpha Zeta Chapter, founded in 1936, of the Zeta Phi Beta sorority included Arnolta Williams, Alpha Hayes Moore, Mamie Lucille Horn Butler, Blanche Jenkins, Waltee McRae Perkins, and Elinor Littlejohn.

These are members of the Eastern Star Organization, a sister group to the Prince Hall Masons.

127

Acknowledgments

This pictorial history is my attempt to capture some of the glory of a community that once thrived in economic prosperity and now has been relegated to fond memories and vacant lots. Much of the old Black Jacksonville has been demolished. But thanks to the personal family photograph collections, most of which contained the rich works of Mr. Ellie Weems and institutional collections, a piece of that history is captured in this publication.

I am deeply indebted to many people who helped to see this book come to fruition. My maternal great great grandfather Henry Casterlow Smith moved his family to Yukon, Florida, from Georgia during the teens. Yukon was a small hamlet located outside of Jacksonville. There my grandmother Lola Pollock married Henry Harris and gave birth to three children, including my mother Deloris Harris. My paternal grandparents James and Elizabeth Mason also came to Jacksonville from Georgia and South Carolina by the early 1920s; they met, married, and gave birth to my father Herman Mason. At the Two Spot Night Club, one night in 1953, my parents met, and the rest, as they say, is history. My Jacksonville ties and roots run very deep.

In the 1960s and 1970s, my summers as a child and youth were spent in Jacksonville surrounded by the nurture and love of many family members. The inspiration of my uncle Henry Harris Jr. and his love for sharing stories of Jacksonville served as the main impetus to develop this book and also the fact that no other pictorial history had been published.

I am especially indebted to my two aunts who kept me filled with fish and clips during the research phase of this book. Yes, clips, not chips. My Aunt Catherine Edwards always cooked fresh fish during my visits to Jacksonville and my Aunt Janie Mason supplied me with a collection of newspaper clippings on blacks in Jacksonville. Her collection was extensive!

I am deeply grateful to my parents, sisters Dionne Bodford and Minyon Conley, and Arthur Conley for his influence in my love for photographs. I would like to extend special thanks to the late Geneva Pollock, Mae Emma Steward, Josephus and Annie Bell Pollock, Claudia Jones, Mamie Blythewood, Jimmy Wideman, Michael Edwards, Debra Glover, Robert Mays, Pat Perry, Jimmy Lanham, Carl and Linda Senior, Carl and Patrice Senior, Clayton and Vivian Senior, Clayton Senior, Cheryna Hamilton, Randy Biggs, James "Bubba" Mason, JoAnn and Harrell Buggs, Kammi Henderson, Harrelyn Buggs, Iralene Dickerson, Walter Odoll, Patricia Dobson, Minnie Thurston, Raiford and Priscilla Brown, Dr. Deloris Muldrow Saunders, Claude Hunter, Ernestine Latson Smith, Gwen and Hattie Stewart, Natalie Hackel Haas, Richard McKissick, Ralph Tisdale, George Rice, Thelma Mitchell, Doris Avery Jones, Thelma Hair Jones, Andria Lang, Dr. Johnetta Cole, Mavynee Betsch, Renee Glover, local author B.J. Sessions, and of course the undisputed historian of Black Jacksonville—Camilla Perkins Thompson. Also, I want to give a very special thanks to Joseph and Loretta Coppock, for their special support of this project; and the Louisiana Street Reunion Committee, including Olivia Forest, John Lewis, Jerome Forest, Henry Williams, Pat Forest Parker, Franklin Smith, Ernestine and Sam Sanders, and Leroy Gore.

Special thanks also go to Eileen Brady at the University of North Florida Library Special Collections; Mr. C.H. Harris at the Haydon Burns Public Library; the staff at the P.K. Young Library at the University of Florida in Gainesville; Isaiah Williams, *Florida Advocate*; Charlotte Stewart, "Social Speaking Column"; Mary and Ericka Simpson, publishers of the *Florida Star Newspaper*, for their support of this project; and Tonya Weathersbee and Sharon Weightman (*Florida Times Union*), for their assistance.

I would also like to thank the staff at Digging It Up: Kevin Johnson, Mozelle Powell, Patrick Stephens, Eric "Bilal" Taylor, and Dexter Weldon, for their assistance on this project and Meteor Photographs, for the reproduction of the photographs. This book is just the tip of the iceberg on the rich history of Black life in Jacksonville. To the next generation: Shakari, Jolaun, Darryl Jr., Kenyondra, Shanquail, Chanel, Janni Marie, and all the unborn generations whose roots are in Jacksonville, this is for you.